DODD, MEAD WONDERS BOOKS include WONDERS OF:

ALLIGATORS AND CROCODILES. Blassingame
ANIMAL NURSERIES. Berrill
BARNACLES. Ross and Emerson
BAT WORLD. Lavine
BEYOND THE SOLAR SYSTEM. Feravolo
BISON WORLD. Lavine and Scuro
CACTUS WORLD. Lavine
CAMELS. Lavine
CARIBOU. Rearden
CATTLE. Scuro
CORALS AND CORAL REEFS. Jacobson and Franz
CROWS. Blassingame
DINOSAUR WORLD. Matthews
DONKEYS. Lavine and Scuro
DUST. McFall
EAGLE WORLD. Lavine
EGRETS, BITTERNS, AND HERONS. Blassingame
ELEPHANTS. Lavine and Scuro
FLIGHTLESS BIRDS. Lavine
FLY WORLD. Lavine
FROGS AND TOADS. Blassingame
GEESE AND SWANS. Fegely
GEMS. Pearl
GOATS. Lavine and Scuro
GRAVITY. Feravolo
HAWK WORLD. Lavine
HERBS. Lavine
HOW ANIMALS LEARN. Berrill
HUMMINGBIRDS. Simon
JELLYFISH. Jacobson and Franz
KELP FOREST. Brown
LLAMAS. Perry
LIONS. Schaller
MARSUPIALS. Lavine
MEASUREMENT. Lieberg
MICE. Lavine
MONKEY WORLD. Berrill
MOSQUITO WORLD. Ault
MULES. Lavine and Scuro
OWL WORLD. Lavine
PEACOCKS. Lavine
PELICAN WORLD. Cook and Schreiber
PIGS. Lavine and Scuro
PONIES. Lavine and Casey
PRAIRIE DOGS. Chace
PRONGHORN. Chace
RACCOONS. Blassingame
RATTLESNAKES. Chace
ROCKS AND MINERALS. Pearl
SEA GULLS. Schreiber
SEA HORSES. Brown
SEALS AND SEA LIONS. Brown
SNAILS AND SLUGS. Jacobson and Franz
SPIDER WORLD. Lavine
SPONGES. Jacobson and Pang
STARFISH. Jacobson and Emerson
STORKS. Kahl
TERNS. Schreiber
TERRARIUMS. Lavine
TREE WORLD. Cosgrove
TURTLE WORLD. Blassingame
WILD DUCKS. Fegely
WOODS AND DESERT AT NIGHT. Berrill
WORLD OF THE ALBATROSS. Fisher
WORLD OF BEARS. Bailey
WORLD OF HORSES. Lavine and Casey
WORLD OF SHELLS. Jacobson and Emerson
WORLD OF WOLVES. Berrill
YOUR SENSES. Cosgrove

WONDERS OF
MULES

Sigmund A. Lavine

& Vincent Scuro

Illustrated with photographs and old prints

DODD, MEAD & COMPANY
NEW YORK

For Eileen—who doesn't need to "look up" why

ILLUSTRATIONS COURTESY OF: American Donkey and Mule Society, 11, 25 *left,* 27, 43 *top,* 45, 46, 47 *top,* 58 *top;* C. W. Bradley, Georgia Mule Association, Chatsworth, Georgia, 13, 23, 34, 48 *top and bottom right,* 60 *right;* British Museum, 17, 18; Colorado Historical Society, 14; Jack Hackethorn, 58 *bottom;* Hawaiian State Archives, 38; Charles Heath, 43 *bottom,* 59; Photo by Nicholas J. Krach, 21; National Archives, 29 *top,* 36, 50, 52, 53, 54; The New Jersey Historical Society, 20, 35; Tom Richardson, 48 *left;* Santa Fe Railway, 37, 39; Vincent Scuro, 6, 9, 10; Norma Talburt, 25 *right;* Norma Talburt, Photo by Jack M. Wildman, 60 *left;* U.S. Army Photograph, 8, 26, 31 *bottom,* 47 *bottom,* 55, 56, 62; United States Borax and Chemical Corporation, 41; USDA Photo, 29 *bottom,* 32; Welcome Swiss Tours, 31 *top.*

Frontispiece by Mike Kops

Copyright © 1982 by Sigmund A. Lavine and Vincent Scuro
All rights reserved
No part of this book may be reproduced in any form
without permission in writing from the publisher
Printed in the United States of America

1 2 3 4 5 6 7 8 9 10

Library of Congress Cataloging in Publication Data

Lavine, Sigmund A.
  Wonders of mules.

  Includes index.
  Summary: Discusses the mule, a hard-working, intelligent animal which is considered one of the greatest successes in the selective breeding of livestock.
    1. Mules—Juvenile literature.   2. Mules—Folklore—
Juvenile literature.   [1. Mules]   I. Scuro, Vincent.
II. Title.
SF362.L38   636.1'8   82-4963
ISBN 0-396-08051-0   AACR2

CONTENTS

1 Meet the Mule   7

2 Lore of the Mule   12

3 Breeding Mules   22

4 Types of Mules   28

5 "They Helped Build America"   33

6 Keeping a Mule   42

7 Mules and War   49

8 "Mulish" Quirks   57

  Index   63

A saddle mule tacked up and ready to go

1 MEET THE MULE

On mules we find two legs behind,
And two we find before,
But we stand behind before we find
What the two behind be for.

Man has been dodging the kick of the mule for hundreds of years. Although ancient writings and inscriptions reveal that the mule was in use before 800 B.C., no one knows for certain when or where it originated. Early Greek literature contains several references to the raising of mules in Cappadocia, the center of modern Turkey, that are confirmed by the Bible (Ezekiel 27:14). Therefore, zoologists theorize that the mule was first bred in Asia Minor. This speculation is confirmed by Anacreon (563–488 B.C.), a Greek poet who credits the Mysians of Cappadocia with being the first to breed mules.

The mule is but one of a long list of animals "manufactured" by man to serve specific purposes. For example, because the early Egyptians required a keen-sighted, swift dog to run down gazelles, they produced the sleek, graceful Saluki. Similarly, English "sportsmen" seeking a compact, courageous dog to fight bulls evolved the malformed Bulldog.

Both the Saluki and the Bulldog were created by selective breeding—mating stock with the required physical characteristics until a definite type is established. Man has not only developed more than five hundred types of dogs by selective breeding but also a large number of specialized breeds of other domesticated animals. While these breeds of cattle, goats, horses, pigs, and sheep have played a most important part in human progress and in the rise of civilization by furnishing food, clothing, and other necessities, few manmade animals are as useful as the mule. Surefooted, strong, smart, and sound of constitution, the mule, which can be used for draft work, pack work, and riding, combines the size of the horse with the endurance of the donkey.

Mules are the offspring of a male donkey (jackass or jack) and a female horse (mare). A well-bred mule has a conformation that gives the appearance of a horse's body on the legs of a donkey. Both horse mules (male mules) and mare mules (sometimes called "molly mules") resemble their sires more than their

A mule has the body of a horse and the ears of a donkey.

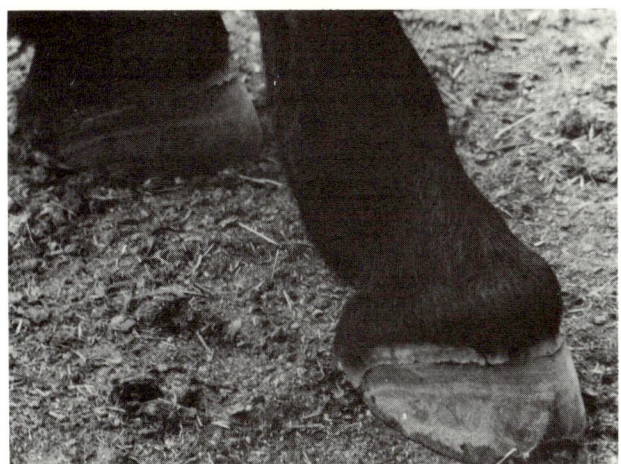

Hoof of a mule is smaller and more oval than that of a horse. Mules usually require shoes.

dams. While the neck and croup (rump) are shaped like those of a horse, the head, ears, tail, and sparse mane look like a donkey's. A mule's back is straighter and flatter than that of a horse, and the withers (the highest point of the shoulders) are poorly defined.

The hoofs of the mule differ from those of the horse, being smaller and more oval in shape. Like donkeys, mules do not have "chestnuts," the callus growths on the inner leg at the knee and hock that are characteristic of horses. While many mules are not as tall as the average horse, they range in size from 12 to 17-2 hands high at the withers. A hand is the unit of measurement used to determine the height of horses, donkeys, and mules, a hand being equal to four inches. Thus the three-foot mini-mules seen in parades and in circus rings are nine hands high and the smallest of all mules. Their dams are pony mares.

Because most mules are solid gray, white, brown, black, or sorrel (a light reddish-brown) and generally do not have stockings (white leg markings), some people think that mules are not as attractive as horses. Mules rarely have a blaze (a broad white mark extending below the nose), but some of them have a white mask over the lower part of the face. Some breeders are producing strikingly colored mules by crossing calico, paint, pinto, and spotted mares with donkeys. Among the most handsome of these are mules with Appaloosa coloration.

Mules can go without food and water for longer periods of time than horses. They can also withstand changes in climate better than horses. But, despite these attributes, the mule is regarded with mixed feelings by man. This is because the mule has an undeserved reputation for stubbornness, stupidity, and sudden bursts of ill temper.

While there is no doubt that mules have strong wills and can be unreasonable, their "stubbornness" is usually due to the fact that a mule will not knowingly put itself in a dangerous position. Horses sometimes rely upon their riders to keep them out of trouble but a mule takes no chances and refuses to "become involved in a situation that, to him, appears hazardous."

Nor are mules stupid. There are those who claim that mules are far more intelligent than horses. These individuals point out that if a frightened horse throws its head up and touches something, it immediately tosses its head even higher, which often causes an injury. But if a mule's ear comes in contact with an object, it quickly lowers its head. Similarly, most horses that run

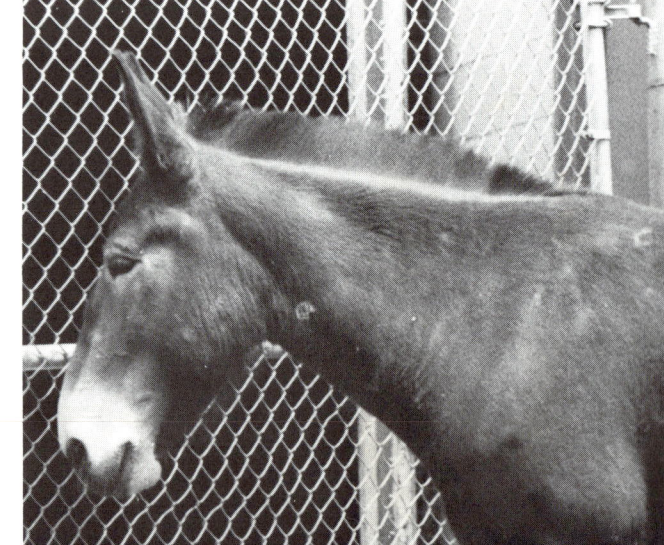

This mule has the characteristic white mask.

An Appaloosa mare and her saddle-mule foal

into barbed wire thrash around, thereby driving the barbs deep into their flesh. The "stupid" mule avoids barbed wire but, if caught, stands still until released. Stockmen also praise the mule for not overeating when it encounters an unlimited supply of food. In the same situation, horses eat until they make themselves sick.

Generally speaking, the highly intelligent mule does not refuse to work, nor does it kick or display any other unattractive trait unless it has been abused, badly trained, or thinks that it is in danger. Experienced handlers of mules insist that "A mule won't kick you unless you deserve it." A mule trainer named Thomas Ireland agrees with this statement and claims that a mule distinguishes between just and cruel punishment. Ireland also warns that a mule "will carry a grudge against a cruel man for as long as it takes to get even."

2 LORE OF THE MULE

Credulous individuals credit the mule with carrying both good and bad luck. As a result, some superstitions featuring the mule are contradictory. For example, while many residents of the southern United States believe that finding a mule's shoe foretells sixteen years of misfortune, Californians maintain that good fortune will come to anyone who picks up a mule's shoe—particularly if it was cast by a white mule.

The gullible credit white mules with magical powers. Not only do they claim that bad luck will haunt the killer of a white mule but also that white mules become other animals after death. Another widespread conviction is the belief that you will marry the first person with whom you shake hands after seeing one hundred white mules. The superstitious are also confident that anyone who kisses his left hand as soon as he sees a white mule will discover a treasure.

Success is sure to come to those who count one hundred mules—white mules equal five of any other color—but it will not arrive until a red gate is passed. It is profitable to wish on a gray mule, providing the right thumb is stuck in the mouth and then used to "stamp" the left hand. Some claim that failure to wet the thumb will prevent the wish from coming true. Another superstition states that a wish made on a gray mule will be granted providing one does not look back after passing the mule.

In Iran, formerly Persia, where ghouls are said to take the form of mules, owners protect their animals from such possession by hanging blue beads on their saddles. To counteract the evil eye, Spanish muleteers fasten a piece of deer horn mounted in iron on the harnesses of the mules they drive. Elsewhere superstition associates the mule with malevolent spirits. Lha-mo, the dreaded Lamaist demon who spreads disease, is always depicted riding a white-faced mule. In Mexico and Costa Rica, mules packing heavy loads of gold are thought to help the Devil snare the souls of greedy men. But these mules are not so diabolical as those that supposedly are the assistants of the sorceresses who cast spells on brides during marriage ceremonies.

Common speech has made good use of the mule. The animal's characteristics—real and imagined—are responsible for numerous idiomatic expressions. Few of these are complimentary, although a football player might be flattered if told he was not only "strong as a mule" but also "tough as a mule," with the

The mule's ability to do hard work gave rise to the expression "strong as a mule." This one is pictured at the Georgia Mule Frolic.

ability "to kick like a Kentucky mule" as well. While "to look as nice as a blue mule" signifies approval, calling someone "a bone-headed mule" is the height of disparagement.

A strong-willed person is reproached by being classified as "obstinate as a mule" or "stubborn as a bobtailed mule." Anyone difficult to get along with is said to be "contrary as a mule" or "balky as a mule." To accuse an individual of being "crazy as a humpbacked mule" is most insulting. But it is even more offensive to tell a singer that he has "the voice of a mule" or that he "brays like a mule."

Many proverbs feature mules. Most of them need no explanation. The meaning of the Chinese "There is no use starving the horse to fatten the mule" is obvious, as is the Moroccan "None but a mule denies his family." Nor is there any difficulty in understanding the cynical Hindu "Friend and mule fail in time of need," or the Greek "He who is too adventurous loses both horse and mule."

Other mule proverbs are more complicated. For example, the Latin *Mutuum muli scabunt* (Mules scratch each other) is the equivalent of the English "Scratch my back and I'll scratch

These 19th-century surveyors' mules appear to be taking turns scratching each other.

yours," inferring that a favor will be returned. In Russia, the statement "A mule's gallop is soon ended" is employed when an individual enthusiastically starts a task but soon stops working. Germans taunt those who put on airs with "Mules brag that their ancestors were horses." The overly critical in Spain are put in their place by being told "He who looks for a mule without fault must go on foot."

The Irish "There are three things that cannot be ruled—a mule, a pig, and a woman" is not subtle. But the meaning of "To shoe one's mule" is hidden. This proverb, widespread in Europe, means to appropriate money or property entrusted to you.

Unlike the donkey and the horse, the mule plays only a minor part in religion. However, Selene, the ancient Greek moon goddess, supposedly rode a mule across the heavens, while the Roman goddess Epona was considered the patroness of the mule and all associated with it.

Christian lore displays little regard for the mule. This is because of the legends that detail the mule's actions on the night Jesus was born. Typical of these accounts is the one told by the Chichicastenango Indians of Guatemala. They claim that the night of the Nativity was extremely cold and, upon seeing the infant turn blue and stiffen, herdsmen drove their stock into the stable. While the cow, goat, horse, ox, and sheep blew their hot breaths over the Child and revived Him, the mule snorted in His face. For punishment—so the Chichicastenango say—the mule has been forced to carry burdens all through history.

Legends also explain why the mule cannot reproduce. In the Azores they hold this is because the mule pulled straw out of the manger in which Jesus lay and ate it. According to the Tepecanos of Mexico, the mule is barren because it threw Mary when she attempted to ride it.

Nevertheless, tradition maintains that, on the island of Rhodes, the Thairey Monastery was built with stones hauled from the quarry at Londos by mules with no human guidance. In Cocullo, Italy, a shoe cast by the mule ridden by the town's patron saint is exhibited in the local church. On the island of Malta on St. Anthony's Day, mules are decked with ribbons and tassels and paraded to church, where they are sprinkled with holy water and blessed.

Although Moslems in Morocco laugh at the clowns that portray mules in the masquerade that takes place during the Great Feast, they have considerable respect for the mule. This stems from their regard for Al Burak, the ancient Arabian symbol of purity. Al Burak is depicted as a lady-faced mule with flowing plumes.

The Faithful believe that one night Mohammed was awakened by Al Burak and was so startled that he knocked over a vessel of water. Mounting Al Burak, Mohammed rode from Mecca to Jerusalem and then through the seven heavens where he spoke to the angels. Upon arriving home, Mohammed discovered he had been away so short a time that the spilled water had not yet reached the floor!

An extremely heavy load of literature is carried by the mule. References to the animal are found in ancient Egyptian texts, Arabic writings, and the Bible. Catullus, Herodotus, Homer, Suetonius, Varro, and other classical authors both praise and abuse the mule. Nor have more modern writers, including Samuel Butler, James Fenimore Cooper, Richard Halliburton, Joel Chandler Harris, Oliver Wendell Holmes, Robert Surtees, and Jonathan Swift, always dealt kindly with the mule. Meanwhile, many poets have ridiculed the mule but, oddly enough, most of them did not sign their work. However, William Faulkner was proud of the graphic description of the physical appearance and personality traits of the mule he presented in his widely acclaimed novel *Sartoris*.

Long before the mule appeared in print it was featured in tribal tales. Mules are the helpful associates of folk heroes in stories told by the Ute Indians and by the Kurds of Turkey. The mule is also the central character in fables recounted by the Hausa in Africa, and it plays an important part in *El Cid*, the romantic chronicle of the exploits of Spain's legendary hero. Pueblo Indians spin yarns in which men are transformed into mules. These tales have much in common with the accounts that appear in the *Arabian Nights* of the witch who turned young men into mules.

One of the most beautiful vases unearthed by archaeologists excavating at Thebes, the ancient capital of Egypt, depicts a chariot drawn by mules. The potter who decorated this vase is

This unusual early Greek vase is decorated with a colorful mule's head. The other side pictures the activities of Dionysus, the wine god, better known as the Roman god Bacchus.

The Greek potter who fashioned this vase made sure all who saw it would realize that a mule was drawing the wedding party—note the ears!

unknown, as are the artisans who painstakingly carved the miniature wooden mules that were buried with the pharaohs. Unknown, too, is the Cyprian sculptor who fashioned and gaily painted a terra cotta model of a wagon drawn by four mules in the fourth century B.C.

Other early nameless artists created representations of the mule out of stone and metal and pictured them on coins. One of these coins was minted by Anaxilaus, the tyrant of Rhegium (494–476 B.C.), to celebrate his victory in the mule-car race at the Olympic Games. Incidentally, mule cars filled with wedding parties are a common motif on Greek vases. So are pictures of Dionysus, god of fertility, riding a mule.

During the Middle Ages when masters of the brush devoted

their talents to painting religious pictures, they often included the mule in their works. This is particularly true of Nativity scenes. Mules also appear in certain illuminated medieval manuscripts containing calendars showing each month's farm chores.

While Goya, Lopez, and other famous artists have painted the mule, they rarely showed it working. This has been done by a number of more modern American painters. Among these are Frederick Remington, who depicted the use of the mule in the Old West, and Thomas Hart Benton, who featured the mule in his series of paintings dealing with rural life.

The *clop* of mules' hoofs can be heard clearly in Ferde Grofé's "Grand Canyon Suite," and the whips of mule skinners crack in "Mule Train." Interestingly enough, the unmusical mule has inspired both famous composers and unknown writers of songs.

Blacks laboring on plantations made up many of the songs sung by those who worked mules. These songs usually were poorly rhymed and had an irregular meter. But they vividly detailed the temperament of the mule and told how it was used. One song, "The Kickin' Mule," became a favorite of "end men" —the comics in minstrel shows—throughout the United States. "Whoa, Mule" was also heard in the theatres. It tells of a balky mule with a hollow tooth and a tremendous appetite.

Miners not only wrote humorous ditties and work songs featuring their mules but also composed tunes lauding them. Throughout the West, miners bellowed "My Sweetheart's a Mule," along with similar compositions. The crude humor of certain of these songs is in direct contrast to the haunting melodies Spanish muleteers sang as they drove their sturdy pack animals from trading post to trading post. English poet Hilaire Belloc captured the spirit of these men in "Tarantella," a poem about an inn in the High Pyrenees frequented by young muleteers who hadn't "got a penny" and "weren't paying any."

A mule "single" pulls a barge on the Morris Canal between Bayonne and Jersey City.

Today in many city schools pupils delight in singing about a mule named Sal who faithfully served her master by drawing barges for fifteen years "on the Erie Canal."

Most domestic animals are important in folk medicine, but not the mule. This is probably due to its poor reputation. Nevertheless, it is said that anyone who kisses a mule will be immune to scarlet fever. Countryfolk claim the best way to get rid of warts is to take some axle grease from the left front wheel of a wagon drawn by a mule and rub it on the warts with a feather from a white turkey. The rubbing must be done exactly at 3:30 p.m. Otherwise the wart will not vanish.

Not only does folk medicine make little use of the mule but also the mule is of slight importance in weather lore, although the residents of North Carolina claim mules' eyes attract lightning. While the ancient Arab astronomers who saw animals, birds, giants, and monsters in the stars did not associate the mule with lightning, they did connect it to the heavens. In their charts they pictured Aquarius (the water carrier, eleventh constellation in the Zodiac) as a mule carrying two jugs of water.

It would take a book many times the size of this one to record how the mule has been accepted and rejected throughout history. Ridden by kings in some lands, the mule was considered an unsuitable mount for nobility in other countries. Thus when the Milanese revolted against Frederick Barbarossa, head of the Holy Roman Empire, they expelled his wife from their city and forced her to ride away sitting backward on a mule. But noble Romans delighted in riding mules. Nero was so proud of his mules that he shod them with silver shoes. The wicked empress Poppaea was even more extravagant—her mules had gold shoes.

Queen Isabella of Spain mounted on a mule. Throughout history, ladies of noble birth, as well as kings, have ridden mules.

3 BREEDING MULES

Because the mule proved so useful, ancient peoples experimented with breeding horses to the onager and other wild asses. The foals produced by these matings—none of which ever occur in the wild state—proved of little value. In more recent years, zebra and horse crosses have been made. Foals from these matings are called zebroids. While zebroids can be used as draft animals on African farms, they inherit the nervousness and pugnacity of their zebra parent.

Crossing a male horse (stallion) and a female donkey (jenny) produces a hybrid known as a hinny. However, hinnies are not as economically valuable as mules. This is because hinnies are smaller than mules and therefore cannot carry as much weight or haul heavy loads. Described as *effrentis et tarditatis* (unrestrained and slow of movement) by the famous Roman naturalist Pliny the Elder, the hinny has never been as popular as the mule except in Ireland. Yet the hinny's stamina and trot make it an excellent mount.

Hinnies inherit their height from their mothers and also their strength and longevity. But they look like their sires. Thus hinnies have smaller ears, longer manes and tails, and a more horselike appearance than mules. While the voice of a mule sounds

In the selective breeding of livestock, the mule is an outstanding success.

like "the gasp of an asthmatic steamboat in distress," a hinny whinnies somewhat like a horse. Most mule owners maintain that each mule and hinny has a distinctive voice that blends the characteristics of the whinny and the bray.

All in all, the mule is one of man's greatest successes in the selective breeding of livestock. But there will be no mules in the future unless they are wanted. This is because male mules are sterile. However, a female mule mated with either a stallion or a jackass *may* produce a foal. Proof that this rarely happens is furnished by the Latin *Cum mula peperit* (When a mule foals), which is the equivalent of the modern expression, "Once in a blue moon."

Similarly, male hinnies cannot reproduce their own kind. If a female hinny is bred to a stallion, she will not foal. Bred to a donkey, her offspring will be a typical donkey.

Centuries before mules set foot in America, Europeans and other inhabitants of the Old World were breeding them. Italian and Spanish breeders were primarily interested in developing sturdy pack mules, while the French concentrated on producing heavy draft mules for farm work.

For many years, the French province of Poitou was the European center of draft-mule raising, some fifty thousand animals being bred annually. Poitou mules, sired by a local breed of long-bodied donkey with exceptionally large legs, were famous throughout the world. In fact, until Americans began to raise mules on a large scale, it was widely held that the Poitou jacks alone possessed the necessary qualifications for producing outstanding mules.

George Washington—one of the first Americans to advocate the use of mules—preferred Poitou stock until he was given a large Spanish male donkey by the King of Spain. Some historians claim Washington named this splendid animal Royal Gift. All agree that Washington placed an advertisement in a Philadelphia newspaper in 1786 stating that his jack was available for stud. In his announcement, Washington not only listed his donkey's good points but also called attention to "the great strength of mules" and to their "longevity, hardiness, and cheap support which gives them a preference of horses that is scarcely to be imagined."

Less than fifty years after Washington's advertisement appeared, American-bred mules were fairly commonplace throughout the United States. Meanwhile, livestock dealers in Charleston, South Carolina, were importing jacks from the Spanish province of Catalonia. There was a brisk demand for these donkeys, which had been introduced into Catalonia by the Moors when they conquered Spain in A.D. 714. The handsome, good-tempered black Catalonian jack ranged in size from 14 to 16-2 hands and was particularly popular in the southern states.

The great American statesman Henry Clay was among the Kentucky planters who bought a pure-blooded Catalonian jack. Clay named his purchase Mammoth Warrior and offered him at stud. Even when female donkeys "entirely destitute of any good quality except hardihood and ability to get a living where any other animal save a goat would have starved to death" were bred to Mammoth Warrior, their foals were outstanding.

Breeding jennies (female donkeys) to Mammoth Warrior was the first step in the evolution of the showy Kentucky mule. The second step was the mating of Mammoth Warrior's female get to Mammoth, a famous Catalonian sire imported by a South Carolina planter. As a result of this procedure, the so-called Kentucky jack evolved. Breeding these male donkeys to well-chosen mares produced the Kentucky mule.

Besides its attractive appearance and good qualities, the Kentucky mule was noted for its courage. No mule was more avidly sought by farmers and, even as late as the 1880's a livestock dealer had no difficulty in selling a Kentucky mule for five thousand dollars.

Left: *Champion donkey, Mammoth type, used for mule breeding.*

Below: *Cracker Jack, a champion donkey, has sired many mules in his time.*

As well as ordering Catalonian and Andalusian donkeys from Spain, mule breeders in Illinois, Indiana, Missouri, and the southern states imported jacks from France, Italy, and Majorca. By breeding and cross-breeding these imported studs with mares having considerable Thoroughbred blood, mules of various size, conformation, and temperament were produced. One of the best known was the well-proportioned, stylish draft mule bred in Missouri. This mule was so highly regarded that buyers in other states would purchase, sight unseen, large shipments of Missouri "smooth mules" from the proprietors of the Mammoth Mule Yards in St. Louis.

Not only did American breeders raise mules with differing physical characteristics but also they developed the native jack. Heavier than the imported European donkeys from which it

One method of shipping mules. The white draft mule is taking it calmly but the one on the right has lost its dignity along with its brow band. It also seems to have too many legs!

A class for small mules at an English show held by the British Mule Society.

was derived, the native jack inherited all the good qualities and attributes of its forebears. Eventually, mule breeders and dealers became convinced that the best mules were those sired by native jacks.

While Americans were rearing mules to meet definite needs, mule breeders in other countries were also developing various types of mules. England specialized in raising small, tough pack mules to haul guns and supplies along winding mountain trails in India and other outposts of the British Empire. South Africans experimented with coaches drawn by mules. Italians evolved the compact Razza jack and produced pack mules with tremendous endurance. In China, a small hardy mule was raised by the thousands to work in mines.

4 TYPES OF MULES

Out of selective breeding of foreign and native stock, Americans have produced various types of mules to perform specific tasks. The popular name for each type indicates the work it was intended to do. Thus mule breeders refer to draft, farm, sugar, cotton, saddle, and pack and mine mules.

Mule breeders generally rank individual animals of each type according to conformation, soundness, quality, and condition. The best mules are categorized as "choice," followed by "good," "medium," "common," and "inferior." The sex of a particular mule has little bearing on its rating. Instead, bone structure, muscling over the loin and hindquarters, and the soundness of the animal's feet are given paramount consideration.

The draft mule is the largest and heaviest of all mules. It stands 16 to 17-2 hands high (5'4" to 5'9") and weighs from 1200 to 1600 pounds. Because of its size, the draft mule is suitable for all types of heavy hauling.

Although the draft mule has long been employed on farms, it is not considered to be very efficient when harnessed to a plow, particularly in hot climates. But it performs exceptionally well when hitched to a wagon. As a result, draft mules were "used to haul loads everywhere from the snows of Antarctica to the superheated desert of Death Valley."

Draft mules hitched to an old-type Army wagon used by the American military during the 19th century

Designed for general farm work, the so-called farm mule is slightly lighter and smaller than the draft mule. Farm mules were originally developed by breeding Thoroughbred stallions to huge Percheron mares, or to mares of other breeds of draft horse, and then mating the fillies born to the mares with native jacks.

A good farm mule

Two types of mules were created for specialized farming. Sugar mules, as the name implies, have worked in sugar plantation fields and hauled harvested cane to the mill. Some mills are mule-powered—a mule either walks in circles tied to a beam fastened to the grinding gears or, mounted on a treadmill, turns a belt. Although sugar mules are as big as draft mules, they are lighter, weighing 1150 to 1300 pounds.

Cotton mules, used in the planting and cultivation of cotton and in the transporting of bolls to the gin, are the smallest and lightest of the agricultural mules.

The saddle mule is the result of a cross between a large, well-conformed jack and a good mare of saddle-horse breeding. Saddle mules are used primarily for recreational purposes such as hunting, racing, or pleasure riding. Some ranchers use them for herding cattle or sheep.

Mules employed for packing and in mines are the smallest type produced by American breeders. Because it is almost impossible to load a tall mule, pack and mine mules are rarely more than 14 hands high. Ideally, they should stand 12 to 13-2 hands and weigh 600 to 1300 pounds. Packers and miners are never as concerned about their mules' appearance as they are about their feet and backs. A pack mule with good feet and a

Old print of sugar mill in Cuba. Note the mule, center.

Mule-riding is a popular recreational activity.

strong back can cover twenty to twenty-five miles a day while carrying a 350-pound load, including the weight of the pack saddle, providing the load is properly balanced and tied. Not that there is any danger of an unbalanced, poorly tied load's sliding to the ground. Mules buck off such burdens almost immediately!

Pack mules serve man well in mountainous terrain. While carrying heavy loads, pack mules can be led or driven, and they are controlled easily by voice because all mules have excellent hearing. Muleteers take advantage of this acute hearing as well as the mule's tendency to accept dominance by an experienced member of its group. Packers do this by placing a "bell mare" in charge of a train. This mule, with a bell fastened around her

Mules have been used to carry ammunition in wartime. A pack mule must be loaded just right or it will buck off its burden.

neck, leads the way, and the mules far in the rear follow their leader in single file, guided by the sound of the bell.

Mine mules—used to haul ore and supplies—are approximately the same size and weight as pack mules. If they were any larger they would find it extremely difficult to pass along a mine's narrow underground shafts. Like pack mules, mine mules must have strong backs and sturdy legs. Equally important is their temperament—mine mules have to adjust to living in semidarkness. Indeed, not too long ago, when there were no laws protecting animals, hundreds of mine mules never saw the sunlight again, once they went underground.

A choice surface mining mule

This small type of mule was used in pit mining.

5 "THEY HELPED BUILD AMERICA"

The first mules to set foot in the Western Hemisphere came from Europe on the same ships that brought the early explorers. Mules packed heavy loads for Coronado, De Soto, Onate, and others journeying into the uncharted regions of the New World. The trailblazers who cut the first paths across North America rode mules "in mountains, over deserts and plains, where forage was scant and water only to be had at long intervals." Mules bore surveyors into canyons and ravines where no other domestic animals could go.

The scores of immigrants who flocked to America during the frontier era relied on mules to perform numerous tasks. Mules helped settlers clear forests and carried materials for building houses, roads, and bridges. Teams of mules pulled wagonloads of pioneers from coastal towns to settlements in the interior.

No animal was better equipped to endure the hardships encountered by early settlers on colonial farms. Initially, small mules were favored for light draft work such as removing tree stumps and pulling plows. As agricultural equipment became heavier and more cumbersome, larger mules were used. Owners of plantations in the South prized these bigger animals for their ability to toil tirelessly in tobacco, cotton, and sugar fields.

Georgia mules of this type are highly prized.

The mule trade was one of colonial America's earliest forms of commerce, and mule traders made a good living. Auctions were held on a regular basis in cities, towns, and frontier outposts. Mules were sold or auctioned individually, in pairs, or in teams of six or eight. A well-trained team of mules brought a higher price than if each animal was sold separately.

By 1800, mules were hard at work in the transportation industry, trudging along the towpaths of America's canals. In those days, boats on canal-connected waterways were a vital link between eastern cities and the interior. On canals such as the Delaware and Raritan of New Jersey and the Erie of New York, mules provided the power to pull passengers, luggage, sand, coal, flour, and ice at a speed of about three miles per hour!

Drawings of this era show small boats being towed by one or two mules. As boats were enlarged to carry more cargo, shipping companies increased their "mule power." Three mules per boat, hitched tandem with the driver riding the last mule, became common practice. Horses were also used to pull the canalboats, but the majority of America's canal companies employed mules. This selection of mules over horses for canal work was probably due to the surefootedness of the hybrids. Additionally, drivers felt that mules were less apt to be panicked by sudden noises.

Since the driver's livelihood depended on the amount of work his mules could do, great care was taken to maintain the animals' health. Tired mules were allowed to rest; thirsty mules were given water or allowed to drink from the canal if the water was clean. Injuries received immediate attention. When the mules weren't working, many were treated as the family pets by the driver's children. While drivers were very often homeless boys, some were married men. Some families lived on the canalboats, except during the winter months in the north when the canal was frozen or drained.

Travel on America's waterways flourished into the mid-1800's.

Mules in New Jersey's canal industry during a rest stop in the early 20th century.

Many settlers who began their journeys west on canalboats towed by mules completed them in mule-drawn wagons. A good pair of mules could pull a fully loaded wagon about fifteen miles in one day.

With the discovery of gold and silver in the West during the middle of the nineteenth century, a tremendous demand for mules was created. Prospectors used them as mounts and pack beasts. Mules also brought fortune-seekers, settlers, and clergy of all faiths to the mining towns that sprang up along the frontier. Sixteen-mule teams hitched to wagonloads of water barrels, beer kegs, and provisions were common sights from Colorado to California.

Many stories of the Old West credit mules with leading their masters to magnificent strikes. Mining tales involving mules abound. The treacherous trail of Bluff Spring Mountain in Arizona is lined with mounds of mule bones. Some say the trail leads to a "lost" gold mine somewhere in the hills. No one knows for sure. How the bones got there is a mystery. One theory is that hundreds of mules, dragging the heavy timbers used in mining, were driven over the trail with extreme cruelty. The mules that died were probably abandoned where they fell, accounting for the mounds of bones.

Still other trails in the Southwest are marked with the sun-

Two methods of hauling water using mules in the Old West

Mules pulled stagecoaches and also helped build America's railways. Here mules move dirt for a railbed in eastern Oklahoma about 1899.

bleached skeletons of countless mules. Tales are told of prospectors who, after running out of food, slaughtered their animals and ate them.

Exhaustion probably took the lives of many of the mules that were used to deliver mail. The "Jackass Express"—a man, a mule, and eighty pounds of mail—brought letters and packages to remote mining camps. It was not uncommon for letter carriers to ride the same mule for the entire run from Independence, Missoui, to Salt Lake City, Utah—a distance of over a thousand miles! The Pony Express, the principal mail service in the West at the time, made trips of similar distance but its riders changed horses at relay stations along the way.

By the late 1850's, stage lines were making regular trips between towns and cities in the West. Many of the coaches used by the Butterfield Stage Lines during this era were drawn by teams of four mules each. The Leavenworth and Pikes Peak Express Company's fifty coaches were pulled by teams of the

37

finest Kentucky mules. These well-trained animals covered 125 miles every twenty-four hours! Through it all they withstood scorching heat and freezing cold, dodging both outlaw bullets and the arrows of hostile Indians.

The outlaws of the West looked upon mules with mixed feelings. Although these animals provided bandits with a cheap method of making a getaway, the territorial peace officers used mules to pull the "tumbleweed wagon"—a rolling jailhouse.

The Indians of the Plains had high regard for the mule and used it to transport everything from buffalo (bison) meat to tepee poles. While some of the mules owned by Indians had been captured on the range or acquired by trading, most had been stolen. The Apaches were excellent mule rustlers. The Comanches raided ranches in Mexico regularly and sold stolen mules all over the Southwest. However, Indians were not the only mule thieves. The merchants from Sante Fe who made annual trips to California where they swapped woolen goods for mules had the habit of "picking up stock for which they had not traded."

Few transit systems are more efficient than Honolulu's. But as this picture of a mule-drawn streetcar shows, rapid transportation is nothing new in Hawaii's biggest city.

Mule-drawn ambulances were common sights in cities during the late nineteenth century. This one belonged to the Santa Fe Railroad.

Mules helped with the reconstruction of America after the War Between the States (1861–65). Whenever new communities sprang up around the country during the 1870's, mules worked even harder. Some towns hitched these animals to ambulances and buses—with various degrees of success. In Philadelphia, teams of a dozen draft mules led by a bell mare drew railroad cars through the city from one station to another.

Mules were also chosen to draw hearses. Undoubtedly the soft, even gait of the mule was considered to be ideal for transporting the body of a departed soul to its final resting place. A draft mule usually pulled the gravedigger's wagon.

During the late 1800's, mules were used to pack barrels of oil from the fields to refineries. The average yield for a rig in those days was "one mule, one barrel, one day." As production increased, mules were hauling wagons loaded with "black gold."

About 1881, the world's largest deposit of borax was discovered in the heart of Death Valley, California, about 165 miles from the nearest rail line. As a result, Americans no longer had to import this mineral from Tibet or Italy. Called the "white gold of the desert," borax has been used in the manufacture of glass, porcelain, enamel, and soap for hundreds of years.

The most economical way to transport borax out of Death Valley—the "hottest, driest, most desolate spot" in the West—was to hitch one team of twenty mules to two 14-ton cargo wagons and a 1200-gallon water wagon.

Only the strongest and smartest mules were chosen to work on the twenty-mule teams. Each mule had to know its own name and was required to respond quickly to commands. In 1880, a pair of mules with these qualifications sold for about a thousand dollars.

Two men were the key to every successful borax venture—the driver and his assistant, the swamper. The mule skinner was paid about $125 per month to drive the team. His swamper received about $25.00 per month to cook, gather wood for fires, and hitch and unhitch the team every morning and evening.

Twenty-mule teamsters dealt with brutal winds, torrid temperatures, and searing sandstorms. However, none of these perils matched the danger they faced whenever they had to travel down a steep hill.

Since it is impossible for twenty mules to hold back three fully loaded wagons (weighing roughly seventy thousand pounds), a mule skinner had no choice but to throw his full weight on the front wagon's brake while the swamper did the same in the rear. If the brakes held, the wagons screeched to a halt at the bottom of the hill. If they *didn't* hold, the team had to be started up at a full gallop, wheeled around *up* the hill, and gradually brought to a halt.

During the five-year period from 1883 to 1889, thousands of tons of borax were transported out of the Death Valley area. Since mules were so closely associated with the transportation of this mineral, Pacific Coast Borax, predecessor to the United States Borax and Chemical Corporation, adopted the twenty-mule team as its registered trademark and corporate symbol. Today, one set of the original twenty-mule-team wagons is still in

Twenty-mule team hauling borax from the remote regions of Death Valley in California, 1880's

running condition and can be seen at the U.S. Borax open pit mine in Boron, California. Two other sets are displayed in Death Valley.

During the early part of the twentieth century, mules were replaced by new sources of power and transportation. Most of the tasks formerly performed by mules are now done by machines. However, not everyone has abandoned the mule. In some parts of the country, mules are employed where mechanical power is impractical or unavailable. Many Americans rely on mules simply because they can't afford to buy mechanical vehicles. Others keep mules as reminders of the "good old days" when mules "helped build America."

6 KEEPING A MULE

More and more Americans are discovering that owning a mule has many benefits. As noted, mules are excellent beasts of burden. They can also be used for recreational activities. Many people say that a mule is as affectionate and loving as a dog. Therefore, some mules are kept as pets.

While it is beyond the scope of this book to present detailed instructions on mule care, here are a few tips for owners.

The decision to purchase a mule should be given a great deal of serious consideration. Remember that owning an animal is a tremendous responsibility. If you keep a mule on your own property, you must assume the burden of its care yourself, but it you board it at a stable, you must pay for its keep. In either case, owning a mule is not an inexpensive undertaking.

Before you decide to buy a mule, do some research. One of the best sources of information is the American Donkey and Mule Society of Denton, Texas. This organization, founded in 1967, publishes a wealth of material on the various aspects of mule ownership. Another good way to find out more about these animals is to talk to professional "mule people"—individuals who earn their living by buying, selling, breeding, or raising mules. Most mule people are more than willing to talk to pro-

Mules come in many sizes. Choose the mule that's right for you.

spective owners. Talking to someone who currently owns a mule is another way to find out more about these animals. Chances are you'll pick up a few tips on how to select the mule that's right for you.

The type of mule you purchase depends entirely on your reasons for buying one. There is no "best" type. If plow-pulling and light draft work are planned, a farm mule should do nicely.

Mules at work in the "good old days." With today's energy crunch, more mules are being employed in farm jobs.

If the animal is going to be used exclusively for recreation, a saddle mule should be chosen. These and other types can be bought directly from a breeder.

Most mule experts suggest that you have a veterinarian inspect your prospective purchase before you assume ownership. A veterinarian is best qualified to determine if the animal is free of disease and digestive disorders. Mules that do not have sound legs and feet or those with a sluggish or stubborn disposition should be avoided.

Although mules have a reputation for being easy to maintain, they do have a number of requirements. Mules must have abundant fresh air and exercise. A barn or other sturdy structure opening to a large paddock or fenced-in pasture is essential. Be sure that the shelter has adequate ventilation and is kept dry. If a mule is going to share its barn with other mules, each one should have its own stall. Harnesses or riding gear may be kept in the barn or in a separate room.

American mule owners generally follow a food and feeding management program similar to that of the horse and donkey. Most of a mule's nutritional requirements can be met with hay or grain. These animals love corn (on the cob or shelled), wheat, oats, and barley. Commercially prepared feeds and vitamin supplements are also recommended.

Raw vegetables, bread, and stale cake can be used for treats. A mule should not be fed directly from your hand because it may bite you accidentally. Instead, place the treat in a dish or pan on the ground and pet the animal gently while it is eating. Your mule will really enjoy it!

There should always be an abundant supply of fresh water near the barn or pasture. A mule won't drink stale or contaminated water, nor will it drink too much and, as a result, become ill. A mule *will* get fat if fed too much and not worked or exercised enough.

Proper care and feeding will result in an animal as healthy and with as glowing a coat as this work mule.

If your mule is used for riding, you will probably need special equipment. Since a mule has a straight back, a breeching or breast collar may be needed to keep the saddle from sliding forward. The mule also tends to carry its rump higher than a horse, which tips the saddle forward. Most tack shops carry all of the necessary equipment for mule riding.

Every animal needs grooming and mules are no exception. When mules sweat, their hair becomes wet and thus accumu-

Rolling in the dirt is the "favorite pastime of every mule that ever lived!"

lates dust. To complicate the problem, mules *love* to roll in the dirt. This activity is terrific fun for the mule but creates a great deal of work for the owner. Use a sharp-toothed currycomb lightly and carefully to remove caked clumps of clay from the coat. A stiff-fibered brush should be used for general grooming. It's best to groom on a regular basis. Not only will your mule be more attractive but also it will love the attention.

Care of the animal's feet should be handled by a qualified blacksmith. A mule should have its teeth checked regularly by a veterinarian. While mules are famous for their resistance to diseases, they do become ill. Any sign of illness or abnormal behavior should be reported immediately to a veterinarian.

While every individual mule has its own unique way of behaving, there are a number of traits common to all. Like most domestic animals, mules are somewhat shy and tend to be a bit wary of unfamiliar things. If you surprise a mule, its natural reaction will be to kick. Therefore, do not approach a mule from behind. Doing so could be a fatal mistake, since mules always look where they are kicking and rarely miss. The best way to approach a mule is to get its attention by speaking to it softly before moving slowly toward it.

If a mule is haltered or harnessed from the time it is a foal,

Care of a mule's feet is important. A mule receives a new pair of shoes from U.S. Army farrier in Italy in 1943.

Right and bottom right: *A mule foal requires patience in training.*

Below: *A mule can be a faithful and devoted friend.*

it will usually develop a gentle disposition. Teaching a foal new things must be done with patience and perseverance. Forcing the animal to do something it doesn't want to do will undoubtably result in failure and frustration for both of you. Remember that mules respond best to kind treatment. They are perceptive and pick up habits—good and bad—very quickly.

Perhaps the real secret to owning a mule is developing a good relationship with the animal. Try to understand your mule's personality and learn what things make it happy. If you do, you'll be rewarded with years of faithful service.

7 MULES AND WAR

The sturdy mule has served man in war as well as peace, doing its "silent but faithful work without hoping for any reward or compensation." As early as the fourth century B.C., mules packed supplies for the armies of Alexander the Great. From 27 B.C. to A.D. 395, Roman generals employed these animals to carry weapons and dispatches throughout the Empire.

More recently, the British made good use of mules in virtually every corner of their empire. Mules packed ammunition and rations across the deserts of Egypt and through the mountain passes of India. The French military also valued these animals. Teams of mules pulled artillery for the army of Napoleon Bonaparte. Contrary to paintings of the era, Napoleon did not ride a white Arabian stallion when he crossed the Alps in 1800. He rode a mule.

No animal is more closely associated with the United States Army than the mule. American military units have worked with mules since colonial times. During the nation's early years, mules helped Army engineers build forts, roads, and bridges. Mules also participated in the construction of Federal buildings including the new capitol in the District of Columbia.

During the early 1800's, pack trains kept the flow of supplies moving to isolated forts along the frontier. Army scouts and couriers used mules as mounts. Mules also carried ammunition and water for the soldiers who served in the Mexican War (1846–48).

However, not everyone at the War Department was satisfied with the use of mules by the Army in the western territories. In 1855, Secretary of War Jefferson Davis (later president of the Confederacy) imported camels to the United States. Davis hoped to prove that these animals were superior to mules for military operations in the desert.

The famous "Camel Experiment" took place in 1856. A camel and mule pack train carrying all of the food and water for a detachment of troops departed from Texas for California. Unfortunately the camels quickly developed aching backs and sore feet from the heavy loads and hard-packed trails. As a result, their cargo had to be transferred to the already burdened mules, which made the rest of the journey packed with double loads!

Some historians credit mules with helping the North defeat

Pack mule and packers near the Mexican border, 1883. Mules carried supplies for military units throughout the West.

the South during the War Between the States. In this conflict, mules were essential to the transportation of supplies from rail lines to troops in the field. Not only did the North have a greater number of mules than the South but also those it had were experienced and well trained. Because of its primarily agricultural economy, the South was forced to keep its best mules working down on the farms and had to rely on young, undisciplined stock for military purposes.

Civilians north and south of the Mason-Dixon Line depended on their faithful mules to take them away from the fighting. It was not uncommon for a frightened refugee—free or slave—to run into a meadow, climb on the back of a peacefully grazing mule, and gallop off to safety!

Over a thousand mules served the United States in the Spanish-American War (1898). Some packed salt, quinine, and bullets to soldiers fighting heat, malaria, and Spanish guerrillas in the hills and jungles of Cuba, Puerto Rico, and the Philippines. Journalists covering the war wrote of how exhausted American troopers applauded the arrival of pack trains loaded with desperately needed supplies.

The Spanish, who also employed mules, realized the importance of these four-legged creatures to the American war effort. Whenever they ambushed a pack train, they shot the mules first, then tried to kill the soldiers.

At the dawn of the twentieth century, mules were working with American military units in various locations around the world. Some, including the mules of the 4th Field Artillery Regiment, were stationed in the Philippines from 1906 to 1907 with America's occupation army. Many of this regiment's mules also took part in the border conflict with Mexico (1916–1917). Two mules called Tom and Jerry comprised a wagon team with the 5th Field Artillery, 1st Division, which saw action along the Mexican border. When the United States entered

A mule hauling supplies on a narrow gauge railway through a forest in France during the first World War.

World War I in 1917, Tom and Jerry traveled to France with the American Expeditionary Force (A.E.F.).

World War I (1914–18) started as a local European dispute, grew into a continental conflict, and eventually became a global war involving thirty-two nations. "The World War," as it was known at the time, was fought from "machines and earthen trenches." Since the fighting covered a tremendous amount of undeveloped territory, motorized vehicles were severely hampered by unpaved roads and natural obstacles such as rivers and mountains. As a result, mules were called upon to assist the transportation and artillery units of the nations fighting in the "war to end all wars."

The number of mules sent to Europe with America's "doughboys" was consistent with the magnitude of the war. Records kept by the Army Quartermaster Corps show that 52,375 draft mules and 9,825 pack mules saw action in this conflict. An additional 40,000 American mules were purchased by Great Britain, France, and Italy to serve with their armies.

During World War I, wounded soldiers were transported by

Mules were important to the transportation units of both sides during World War I. A team of mules pulls a truck out of a river in France.

mule-drawn ambulances from the battlefield to aid stations behind the lines. From there they traveled by motor ambulances to hospitals in the cities. However, these "motors" could travel only on dry roads. Thus, when it rained, the mules made the entire trip. Further, whenever a truck got stuck trying to cross a river, the reliable, surefooted mules were called upon to pull it out!

In France, mules pulled food-laden cars on narrow-gauge railroad tracks through densely forested areas. They also hauled rolling kitchens to infantrymen in the field. Pack mules carried

A pair of mules pulls a rolling kitchen. Mules could travel to places where automobiles and trucks could not go.

Mules carried bread in bags and coffee in cans to American doughboys during World War I.

hot coffee and stew in marmite cans and brought bread in bags to doughboys fighting in mountain areas. One company of the A.E.F.'s 3rd Battalion was camped in an area where trucks could not go because their noise might alert the enemy. Under the cover of darkness, pack mules carried hot meals to the men.

Many veterans of World War I feel that mule skinners and the animals they affectionately called "jarheads" are the unsung heroes of that conflict. When a camp was shelled, infantrymen could dive for cover, but the skinner and his team had nowhere to hide. Nor were mules immune to the injuries inflicted by machine guns and poison gas. A mule injured in combat was

This mule was injured by shrapnel and poison gas. It was taken to an aid station where it was treated like a wounded soldier.

Mules have been used to transport troops in wartime for centuries. A mule hitched to a captured Japanese ammunition wagon is used by three members of the 253rd Quartermaster Pack Company on the Burma Road.

taken to a dressing station by a member of an infantry unit and there treated like a wounded soldier!

The introduction of jeeps and other four-wheel-drive vehicles after World War I drastically reduced the number of mules used by the American military. Nevertheless, mules saw action with the United States Army in World War II (1941–45). Over thirty thousand mules were purchased by the Army for duty in the war-torn areas of Italy, China, and Burma.

Muleskinners of the 2nd Battalion, 475th Infantry Regiment, lead mules across a swift river in Burma during World War II. Mules are excellent swimmers.

"Airborne Anne" helps American soldiers lay field wire in Lebanon. The tiny mule was purchased in Beirut for twenty dollars.

During the 1950's, the United States Army replaced almost all of its mules with mechanized vehicles. Other nations did the same. Today most of the world's armies keep mules for parades, as mascots, and as reminders of a bygone era. However, mules have not retired completely from combat duty. During the 1980's, many of the freedom fighters in Afghanistan were able to outwit the invading army of the Soviet Union by riding their mules into mountainous areas where Russian jeeps, tanks, and helicopters could not follow.

8 "MULISH" QUIRKS

During the latter part of the twentieth century, the high cost of fuel for motorized vehicles has brought about a resurgence of interest in mules. As a result, modern mules have added a few "mulish" quirks of their own to the almost legendary reputation of their predecessors.

In many parts of the world, mule-back trips are very popular. Tourists who ride in Switzerland's mule safaris have a chance to see the magnificent Alps with their famous larch forests and meadows full of flowers. Occasionally riders must restrain their mounts from dining on the luxurious vegetation. Mules love to snack, especially in the company of other mules. The Swiss say that these animals are "frugal, untiring, surefooted, and possessing a strong character"—qualities perfectly attuned to life in the Alps.

Participants in riding tours of the Grand Canyon have their breaths taken away figuratively and literally, thanks to their mule mounts. While they are overwhelmed by the fantastic views from mule back, riders may be overcome by the odor of mule droppings. When one mule stops for a "break," all the rest of the mules do, too!

Pancha, a Hawaiian mule, does tricks to entertain children.

Few animals are more entertaining than mules. It has been said that mules love to clown around, particularly those that participate in circuses, rodeos, and wild West shows. The Georgia State Mule Frolic Show, held each October in Chatsworth, consists of buggy-, plow-, and wagon-pulling contests, as well

Mules on display at the Missouri State Fair in 1978

A pair of iron-gray Missouri mules photographed on the farm of Charles Heath in 1945. Mule owners take pride in their animals.

as other mule-related events. "Mule Days" in Bishop, California, a three-day celebration dedicated totally to these animals, is held every Memorial Day weekend. The festivities include racing and packing contests, an auction, and a parade.

For some mules, performing in front of people means "show business." During the 1950's, Francis, the Talking Mule, co-starred with Donald O'Connor in a series of motion pictures. The wise-cracking Francis usually had the last word. A cartoon mule always has the last laugh on the "Hee Haw" television show. Real mules have appeared in countless other TV shows and ads.

Mules also put their best hoofs forward at state fairs. These exhibitions take place over several days and include events such as the four-mule hitch, two-mule hitch, "unicorn" (one mule) hitch, and halter showing. First-place winners in all events usually compete for the title of Grand Champion of the fair.

Charles W. Heath of King City, Missouri, who first exhibited mules in 1937 and has been the Superintendent of Horse and

Left: *Norma Talburt riding Cracker Snap over a cross-country course. Mules are relatively new to this sport.*

Right: *Mule racing at the Georgia Mule Frolic.*

Mule Shows for the Missouri State Fair, says the air in the barns on show day "is filled with excitement." The mules are washed, brushed, rinsed, and sprayed with conditioner to make their coats glisten. Hoofs are polished; tails and manes are trimmed. Naturally the animals are watered, fed, and exercised.

The actual showing takes place in a ring where the exhibitor "tries all sorts of antics to make his mule look good." Exhibitors have been known to "holler, yell, wave caps or hats, crack whips, rattle cans, wave jackets" or anything that will get the entry to hold its head and ears up. Contestants who do not do well in the show try to correct their mistakes and have their mules in better condition for the next year's fair.

Some mules are famous for their ability to leap "from precarious perches to places they cannot see." Stories are told of an Army mule named Hambone that could jump over fences five feet high. Farmers tell of mules that leap out of their corrals to dine on pasturage, jumping back in when they are full! Hunters are thankful for the tough, pony-sized mules they ride while raccoon hunting. "Coon-jumpin'" mules save them the drudgery of having to climb over the seemingly endless number of fences in the Old South's pastures and fields.

Mules have a jumping style all their own. Most do not take a running start when they jump. A coon-jumpin' mule leaps flat-footed—if it decides to jump at all! In some cases, a mule will approach a fence, study it, then casually walk to the nearest gate!

Until recently, people thought that mules could not compete in cross-country jumping, a popular event at many horse shows. This type of jumping is considered to be one of the most difficult equestrian events. The rider and his mount are required to cover a great distance, leaping over barricades along the way.

Most people felt that mules simply did not have the endurance or ability to meet the challenge of cross-country jumping. But, in 1981, Cracker Snap, a five-year-old molly mule bred, raised, and ridden by Norma Talburt of Roseburg, Oregon, participated in this event at several horse shows. Each time, she performed "as well or better" than the horses she competed against.

Preparing Cracker Snap for cross-country jumping required years of hard work and practice. She began her endurance training when she was three years old. By age four she was taught how to jump. Undoubtably some of Cracker Snap's ability was inherited from her parents. Her sire, Cracker Jack, is one of the top producers of mules in the country. (See page 25.) Her dam is an Appaloosa mare.

The endurance possessed by some mules is also well known. In 1976, riders of 175 horses and five mules were entered in a race from Frankfort, New York, to Sacramento, California—a distance of about 3200 miles. When the race was over ninety-eight days later, the winner, riding a Missouri mule, crossed the finish line seventy-five miles ahead of another mule and rider. *They* were several miles ahead of a man on an Arabian stallion!

Modern mules bred for racing are generally the offspring of Thoroughbred mares and American jacks. A racing mule's behavior on the track can be somewhat unpredictable. On any given day it simply may decide not to run. As a result there is no science to betting on these contests. Instead, wagerers place side bets on which mules *won't* come out of the starting gate!

Today's mules get their "kicks" in other sports as well. Three mules, heirs of a tradition dating back to 1899, serve as football-team mascots for the Corps of Cadets at the United States Military Academy at West Point, New York. The present Army mules—Buckshot, Spartacus, and Ranger—attend all home football games, the annual Army-Navy game in Philadelphia, and other "away" games. The mule was chosen to be Army's mascot because of its "strength, heartiness, and perseverance—symbolic of the Corps of Cadets."

There is no question that the many qualities of mules—as well as their "mulish" quirks—have made them valuable allies of man. There is no doubt that mules will continue to be useful in work or play for centuries to come.

The mule is the official mascot of the United States Military Academy at West Point. This one is named Buckshot.

INDEX

Al Burak, 16
American Donkey and Mule Society, 42
Anacreon, 7
Anaxilaus, 18
Antarctica, 28
Arabian Nights, 17
Arabs, 21
Art, 18–19
Asia Minor, 7
Azores, 15

Barbarossa, Frederick, 21
"Bell mare," 31–32
Bible, 7
Bonaparte, Napoleon, 49
Borax, 39–40
Bulldog, 8

"Camel Experiment," 50
Cappadocia, 7
Catalonian jack, 24–25
Clay, Henry, 25
Coronado, 33
Costa Rica, 13

Davis, Jefferson, 50
Death Valley, 28, 39–41
De Soto, 33
Donkey, 8–9, 15, 22, 23, 24–26, 62

Egypt, 7, 17, 49
Epona, 15
Erie Canal, 34–36

Francis, The Talking Mule, 59

Georgia State Mule Frolic Show, 58–59
Guatemala, 15

Heath, Charles W., 59–60
Hinny, 22, 23
Holy Roman Empire, 21
Horse, 8–11, 15, 22, 29

Idioms, 13–14
India, 40
Indians, 15, 17, 35
Ireland, Thomas, 11

Jackass, 8, 23, 62. *See also* Donkey.
"Jackass Express," 37
Jenny, 22, 25. *See also* Donkey.
Jerusalem, 16

Kurds, 17

Lha-mo, 13
Literature, 7, 16–17, 19

Malta, 16
Mammoth Mule Yards, 26
Mammoth Warrior, 25
Mecca, 11
Medicine, 20–21
Mexico, 13, 15
Missouri State Fair, 60
Mohammed, 16
Moors, 24
Morocco, 16
Moslems, 16
Mule
  breeding, 22–26
  care of, 42–48
  color, 9–10
  conformation, 8–9, 28
  constitution, 8, 10, 61–62
  cotton, 28, 30
  draft, 28
  farm, 28, 29, 30, 43
  French, 24
  heavy, 31, 33
  hoofs, 9
  "horse," 8
  intelligence of, 10–11
  Italian, 24, 27
  jumping, 60–61
  Kentucky, 25, 28
  and man, 7–8, 21, 38
  mine, 27, 28, 30, 32
  Missouri, 26
  "molly," 8
  pack, 27, 28, 30–31, 36
  Poitou, 24
  saddle, 28, 30, 44, 45
  showing, 59–60
  Spanish, 24
  sugar, 30
  temperament of, 10–17, 46–48, 57
  in trade, 36
  voice, 22–23
  in war, 49–56
"Mule Days," 59
Mysians, 7

Native jack, 26–27
Nero, 21

O'Connor, Donald, 59
Olympic Games, 18
Onager, 22
Onate, 33

Pliny the Elder, 22
Poitou jack, 24
Pony Express, 37
Proverbs, 14–15

Razza jack, 27
Religion, 15–16
Rhodes, 16
Romans, 21

Saluki, 8
Satan, 13
Selene, 15
Spanish-American War, 51
Stage lines, 37–38
Superstitions, 12–13

Talbury, Norma, 61
Thebes, 17

United States Military Academy, 62

War Between the States, 39, 50–51
Washington, George, 24
World War I, 52–55
World War II, 55

Zebra, 22